CREATING A THERAPEUTIC CULTURE OF MEN

FREEDOM

PRESENTED BY

LINDA D. LEE, PCLC, CCM

Award-winning author of *In Bed with a Snake*

FREEDOM

CREATING A THERAPEUTIC CULTURE OF MEN

Copyright © 2018 LINDA D. LEE

All rights reserved.

No part of this book may be reproduced, distributed or transmitted in any form by any means, graphics, electronics, or mechanical, including photocopy, recording, taping, or by any information storage or retrieval system, without permission in writing from the publisher, except in the case of reprints in the context of reviews, quotes, or references. Request for permission should be addressed in writing to LL Media Group, LLC; Attn: Linda D. Lee, CEO; P.O. Box 6305, Fort Worth, TX 76115.

Scripture quotations marked (NKJV) are taken from the Holman Study Bible NKJV Edition, Copyright © 2013. Used by the permission of Holman Bible Publishers, Inc., Nashville, Tennessee. All rights reserved.

Printed in the United States of America

ISBN: 978-0-9979068-2-0

THER·A·PEU·TIC

adjective

1. Relating to the healing of disease.

Source: Oxford Dictionary

"And the disease men need to be healed from is SILENCE. No longer will trauma be the disease stealing the voice of men in any community. FREEDOM reigns!"

-Linda D. Lee

Table of Content

Introduction.. 1
Men Experience Trauma Too
–and Get Healed!
by Linda D. Lee
A Daughter's Love.. 2
Bloodline Breakers... 5
Voiceless.. 5
His Siblings.. 6
Suppressed Memory.. 7
Purity Is Power Conference........................... 8

A Call for Justice!.. 13
George Washington Carver High School
by Joe Bridgewater
Long Walk Home.. 14
Seventy Year Secret....................................... 18
Confession... 19
Military Life... 19
Epiphany.. 20
Hospital Visit... 21
Your Charge.. 23

Unbound: Breaking the Chains............ 27
by Bruce Lee
Prison Life/Death................................ 28
Seeking Help....................................... 29
Functioning Alcoholic......................... 30
Loving Mentality................................. 30
Role Model... 32
Latchkey Influencers.......................... 33
My Heart's Desire............................... 34
Reality Check...................................... 35
Diabetes: Silent Killer......................... 36
A Mother Cannot Replace a Father.... 37
Speak Life... 40
Other Women..................................... 41
Parental Challenge............................. 43
Guilt and Shame................................. 46
Prayer Changes Things....................... 47
A Father's Rights................................ 50
Revelation.. 55
Regaining Balance.............................. 56
Got My Swag Back.............................. 58
Coping Mechanism............................. 59
Self-Care Is Critical............................. 65
Call to Action...................................... 68
7 Stages of Emotional Adjustment.... 73
Forgiveness...76

FREEDOM

And they overcame him by the blood of the Lamb and by the word of their testimony, and they did not love their lives to the death.

- Revelation 12-11 (NKJV)

Introduction

Men Experience Trauma Too –and Get Healed!

By Linda D. Lee

In a world where society paints a picture that men are afraid of counseling, therapy, psychologists, or psychotherapists... let alone healing, here comes FREEDOM. This book contains strategies into creating a therapeutic culture for men. Believe it or not, men really want to be better communicators to their family and share their traumatic life experiences. One problem; you may need help. FREEDOM is here to help and will reveal simple strategies to restore your voice.

Allow me to take you on a journey of supernatural healing and forgiveness lived out in the 1947 cotton trailer secret of Joe Bridgewater. Then, travel with me in time to meet another overcomer, Bruce Lee, whose penitentiary murder mystery will BLOW YOUR MIND!

Two men. Two different stories. Two different mindsets while conquering trauma.

FREEDOM

FREEDOM is a unique personal development tool presented through the eyes of two male influencers from diverse backgrounds "shaken" by trauma. Their stories will inspire you to heal, forgive, and be free in life, business, or career.

A Daughter's Love

It was a rainy Friday morning, and the road was full of traffic. I was on my way to the "Purity Is Power Conference," in Houston, Texas under the leadership of Pastor Dr. Phyllis Fuller. The closer I got to Houston, the harder it rained. The roads were full of puddles of water as I stayed focused on the road. At a time, I thought of pulling over or slowing down. I was singing, worshipping, and praising God in bumper-to-bumper traffic. Most people travel Interstate 45, but I have never been comfortable traveling that route…until that day. Needless to say, I remained focused and made my way to Houston in record time. As I approached the city limits, a text came across my phone stating that my father had been taken to the hospital… the car went silent. Although the music kept playing, I could not hear it at that moment. I kept staring at my phone, as if I had read the message incorrectly. If you are anything like me, anytime you hear your parents are ill, taken to the hospital, or need anything, etc., that prompts an immediate response. Not that I did not believe God, please. I believe God's report about everything in my life. Simply put, the message caught me off guard.

Prior to leaving home, I did not share with many people my concerns regarding my father's health. I love my father and have such admiration for him, but his health has always been a matter of concern to me. I simply kept a brave face about his whole ordeal and tried not to pester him. But inside, I never liked the way he took his health for granted. I had become accustomed to hearing my mother say that he had another doctor's appointment. Yet, I was hoping that nothing would happen while I was out of town.

There was something different about this trip to Houston. I felt an urgency to get there. Sophia Ruffin was scheduled to speak. I had been following her on social media and trusted the God in her. Everything I watched on her periscope handle pulled me closer to knowing more and more about her. I did not understand why, although I understand now. I cannot explain my reaction to what was revealed. Except, I knew that if the Holy Spirit had me following her, there was a specific reason. I know you're probably wondering who Sophia Ruffin is. Sophia Ruffin is an ordained prophet and the author of the book, "From Point Guard

FREEDOM

to Prophet." She was a famous point guard personality that had been delivered from homosexuality. Since our initial meeting, she has written many holistic tools to help people overcome that lifestyle and be made free. In her book synopsis, "She takes you behind the scene of women's basketball, exposing the shocking connection between women's sport and homosexuality... Sophia reveals how childhood trauma opened the door to perversion and set the stage for same-sex attraction later in life." After watching some of her testimony scopes, I was intrigued to learn more about her ministry. Not because I was confused about my orientation, simply because she always mentioned that the purity conference would bring great revelation to generational curses. There was going to be an impartation for bloodline breakers.

"Love suffers long and is kind; love does not envy; love does not parade itself, is not puffed up; does not behave rudely, does not seek its own, is not provoked, thinks no evil; does not rejoice in iniquity, but rejoices in the truth; bears all things, believes all things, hopes all things, endures all things. Love never fails."

- 1 Corinthians 13:4-8a (NKJV)

Bloodline Breakers

According to Vocabulary.com, "Your bloodline is your heritage or ancestry. In other words, your bloodline includes your parents, grandparents, great-grandparents, and so on." Any person that severs demonic attachments transferred to their bloodline or in a bloodline is a bloodline breaker. They refuse to allow the enemy to continue to keep them bound by generational circumstances and/or sexual sin. I was an overcomer and a bloodline breaker! I had broken sexual sins off my life, but I wanted my father and other men in the family to be free. Can you imagine being bound for years and not having a voice or having it stolen? Some of the men in our family were bound, and others are still bound mentally. And it hurts my heart as a wife, mother, daughter, and aunt to not be able to reach them.

Voiceless

My father was always a soft-spoken and a humble man, but I have always felt there was something else he might have wanted to say or do in life. He was too quiet! Unfortunately, sometimes when he finally decided to speak up, his voice was drowned out. When your voice is never really heard, you slowly shut down from communicating. Never in a million years would I have tied his progress and kept it internally shut down with events from his past. Have you ever desired more for someone but could not explain to them how to obtain it? Well, I have. I wanted my father to have everything his heart desired. Unfortunately, I wasn't sure he wanted it as bad as I did. Let me explain.

His Siblings

I only remember a few of my uncles; I never really developed a relationship with my aunts. Even as a child, I could see how estranged their whole family really was. Yes, like most families, they came together at funerals. Outside of that, we never really saw them. Except for the two younger uncles. We saw them a lot of time! Especially, when they needed something from my father. I could not help but feel that something was not right about my family. Unfortunately, I could not put my finger on it nor was I trying to judge anyone. I just wanted to understand who they were and why we all acted the way we did. I knew some of the members of the family had been promiscuous and had many proclivities, but there was something else WRONG! To me, it seemed like everything was a "family secret." Believe me when I say, I was SICK of family secrets.

Have you ever heard the saying, "Leave the past in the past" ... "That does not concern you" ... "Let dead dogs lie?" To me, they were just all excuses not to face the past and pretend everything was fine. When actually there was a generation of people being eaten up inside, and they did not even know it. My father was one of those people. He had experienced a traumatic incident that began to surface after he read my book, "In Bed with a Snake." Unfortunately, one significant experience many people overlook when it comes to trauma is suppressed memories. My father was right in the middle of one and did not know either.

Trauma

"A deeply distressing or disturbing experience."

-Webster's Dictionary

Suppressed Memory

He shared with me what happened when he was young. He also shared that when he was reading my book and the accounts of my rape he had felt like, "Where have I heard this before?" When he first told me, I thought he meant he had read my book twice. Actually, he meant that the "memory" of being raped sounded familiar. In his mind, he was trying to make the connection with what had happened to him as a child. Reading my book triggered a suppressed memory in him. Unfortunately, I was preoccupied with my own issues that I missed the signs. He was crying out for help silently in a different way. Has anyone ever come to you for help and you missed the signs? It's not a good feeling, is it?

"Purity Is Power" Conference

My father's health kept fluctuating. He was in and out of the hospital. On that day, in particular, I arrived Friday to attend the Purity Is Power Conference. It was a two-day event set to span Friday, August 19th & 20th, 2016 under the leadership of Apostle Phyllis Fuller. Ambassador Sophia Ruffin was one of the guest speakers. I was right on the outskirts of town when a text came through stating that my father had been rushed to the hospital. Prayers immediately went up. Now I am faced with making an impactful decision...do I stay or turn around and return home? Within minutes, the decision was made for me when another text came through my phone. It read, "We'll take care of Dad and see you after the conference." Since I was convinced everything would be fine, I went on to my hotel and rested. I was still concerned about my father, but I knew there was a PRESSING in my spirit to get to this conference. My father was in the best hands possible – God's.

God had something special for me at "this conference," and I had to get there!

Have you ever been so hungry to get somewhere and receive either insight, knowledge, or revelation on something that was going to help you deal with life circumstances? Well, I had that feeling. So, I stayed and attended the conference. Sophia Ruffin was up teaching, ministering generational curses, and there was an anointed atmosphere of liturgical dancers, as well. Most importantly, the atmosphere was set for healing and deliverance.

As the day went on into the next afternoon, Sophia Ruffin began to prophesy and pray for those that came to the altar. Some other people and I accepted the altar call. We were ready to receive all God had for us. As she walked heavy in the spirit, she was led in my direction; the spirit passed me by. I could feel the wind of glory on my arms and in the atmosphere. I stayed at the altar, prayed, and interceded on behalf of "my own family." Not knowing that the spirit was leading her back in my direction. She laid hands on me and began to pray and prophesy. In her prophecy, she broke the generational curses off me and mentioned my father. I knew then that it was the Holy Spirit setting me free. He had a word especially for me regarding my father.

See, I did not share with her or anyone there what was going on in my family. Also, I did not mention to anyone why I was there in attendance, that my father had been rushed to the hospital or the different things that had transpired in my life. A real prophet or prophetess can pick that up in the spiritual realm. So, after she laid hands and prophesied, I felt a lift in my spirit. I knew that I had been made free. One thing she mentioned led me to re-examine the way that I was covering my family in prayer. You know how you think you are praying specifically? Well, after her teaching it was revealed that I could be even more specific. An adjusted prayer has more targeted power than one that misses the mark.

After the conference, I spent time in the presence of God. Seeking Him on what I needed to do next regarding my family and what I had just experienced. What the Holy Spirit told and showed me was that I needed to go to my father's bedside and speak to him regarding his past. He gave me a strategy to use to release my father from his past and generational curses which had been tormenting him for over seventy years. And that was exactly what I did. The story picks up where my father's voice was restored as he gave accounts of his 1947 traumatic accident regarding some neighborhood children. As you visualize his story, also picture him grasping to share "each" word. He has been through a lot in his lifetime! I have never witnessed anyone fighting so hard to let their voice be heard while being short of breath. I believe sharing his story restored some life back to him. In turn, he will impart unto you.

Behold, I give you the authority to trample on serpents and scorpions, and over all the power of the enemy, and nothing shall by any means hurt you.

- Luke 10: 19 (NKJV)

FREEDOM

"So I will restore to you the years that
The swarming locust has eaten,
The crawling locust,
The consuming locust,
And the chewing locust,
My great army which I sent among you.
You shall eat in plenty and be satisfied,
And praise the name of the
Lord your God,
Who has dealt wondrously with you;
And My people shall never
Be put to shame.
Then you shall know that I am
In the midst of Israel:
I am the Lord your God
And there is no other.
My People shall never be put to shame."

-Joel 2:25 (NKJV)

A CALL FOR JUSTICE!

George Washington Carver High School

By Joe Bridgewater

Back in those days, when I was a youngster, the county seat was Alvarado, Texas. Now, the county seat is Cleburne, Texas. So, now the county courthouse was formally the courthouse. It was transformed into the black schoolhouse, which was the high school and the elementary all mixed together. George Washington Carver High School was an all-black school for colored students. Everybody went to school in one building. It was a two-story building that contained no running toilets. If you wanted to go to the bathroom, you had to go outside to the toilets, located at the edge of a field. Of course, that building was torn down, and a single-level "L shaped" building was erected. It had running toilets... so they say, a kitchen and a library. The library was just a small room that had some books in it, but in those days, you did not get the real stuff. You got leftovers. What we got, we thought was "high cotton." Actually, it was stuff they did not want. The stuff was outdated. It is recorded in history that whites handed down things they didn't want any more to black people and colored schools. When white schools got new stuff, colored schools got their old stuff.

High Cotton

"The term "high cotton" or "tall cotton" originates from the rural farming community in the antebellum (pre-Civil War) South when "high cotton" meant that the crops were good and the prices, were, too. The term has generalized to mean one is doing well or is successful."

- Wiktionary. org

Long Walk Home

In the fall of 1947, I woke up and decided to walk to my brother's house and watch TV, but I did not make it. I was headed for the school as I entered the black part of town. Let me draw you a diagram.[i] The road curved, which is a short curve in the vicinity of the old bulldozed two-story high school, which now is an L-shaped school across the way. My brother lived next door to the school I used to go to. As I was walking, I bumped into three neighborhood boys coming from the opposite direction. Another boy was playing around in the cotton trailer. He looked up, saw me, and called me over. I didn't think anything about it - so I went over. We got to playing around in the cotton trailer, and the other boys joined in... and then it happened. They held me down and violated me. It didn't start out like that, but that's how it ended. After it was all over, everyone got scared when they saw blood. They took out up the street, and I was trying to figure out what really happened. I was around 12 years old. It started as a playful prank until it got nasty. They left me in the buggy of cotton. It was one of those buggies that the horses pulled. I was scared to go to my brother's house.

I made my way back to my house and got undressed. My mother knew something out of the way happened. She came over and hugged my neck and asked if I was all right. Of course, at that age, I didn't know what had happened, but I did know something outrageous had happened. I did not know how to articulate to her what had happened to me. My mother thought maybe we had been fighting in the cotton trailer and it got out of hand but actually, two boys held my legs, and the other two boys held my arms. I was faced down when one of them violated me. Afterward, the rapist vanished, and the two brothers went back up the street. I never went to my brother's house again; I was too embarrassed. Instead, I made my way back to my house silently.

FREEDOM

Eventually, I told two of my brothers what happened. They heard me, but they were not really listening to me. They acted like it was no big deal. And, I am embarrassed to admit, I did not even know what happened to me was called "rape" until I got much older.

Male rape - Medical definition:

*<u>Unlawful</u> sexual activity and usually sexual intercourse carried out <u>forcibly</u> or under threat of injury against the will usually of a female **or** with a person who is beneath a certain age or <u>incapable</u> of valid consent.*

- Merriam Webster

---

[1] Diagram included nearby church, candy store, laundry mat, his sister's house, cotton trailer, home of his neighbors, and the predators.

CREATING A THERAPEUTIC CULTURE OF MEN

Statutory rape

Sexual intercourse with a person who is below the statutory age of consent.

One in six women and one in thirty-three men will experience attempted or completed rape in their lifetime.

In eight out of ten rape cases, the victim knows the perpetrator.

Sexual assault is never the victim's fault.

Some assaults occur in public spaces with multiple witnesses.

Some assaults are motivated by hostility, power, and control.

Men can be and are victims of sexual violence. Approximately one in six men will be a victim of sexual violence at some point in their lifetime. Being a victim of sexual violence does not make a man less "manly" and does not have implications for his sexual orientation.

---

1 out of every 10 rape victims are male.[2]

FREEDOM

Seventy Year Secret

This secret was kept over seventy years before it surfaced. I never told anyone else until the suppressed memory began to surface after reading my daughter's book about her rape. She was the first, last, and only person I had even bothered to mention it to lately. I did not share this with my baby sister or baby brother on account of how embarrassed I felt. For a long time, I **hated** the ground those boys walked on because of what they did to me. Gradually, after we moved away to Childress, Texas, the incidents started going away, but the hurt did not go away. It took a long... long... long... time for me to even think about girls in any way. I was a wallflower. I went to school picnics, school athletic prom and kept to myself because I felt dirty... I felt used. They call it rape. All I knew, this did not happen in a small town. Fast forward.

---

2 Source: National Institute of Justice & Centers for Disease Control & Prevention website. Source: Department of Justice website.

Confession

I never told my wife what happened to me. Some might have thought I would have shared this with my older daughter since we talked a lot. She was more along the educational lines. My middle daughter, Linda, was a party girl. My son was a party man. I did not have a reason to bring it up to him. But, what I go through now, no one can ever understand. This book brought back a lot of ancient memories or bad memories I had suppressed. Now when the time comes for me to go to the doctor for a colonoscopy or anything, I get VERY uncomfortable.

Military Life

When I went into the military and had to get a colonoscopy, I always asked them, "Do you really have to do that?" What a real shock after being in the military for four to five years! Although this procedure and others were necessary, I did not enjoy getting them done. They brought back a flood of vivid memories... vivid thoughts. I still did not talk about "the incident" with anyone that would really listen. I remember thinking, only boys and girls engage in intercourse. But once I entered the military, I found out that men being raped was normal.

FREEDOM

Epiphany

As I sat and recalled the details of my story, my daughter, Linda, brought something to my attention; all of the individuals that raped me were dead. She said, "I remember having a conversation with you previously. You were crying, seemed very sad, and asked why was I still living?" She told me God still had something for me to do. Now I understand. God spared my life in order to assist someone else with their story of becoming a survivor. Grace and mercy kept me all those years. Now they will keep you. This book will help men, especially, that have been raped, violated, have suppressed memory, anger, bitterness, or unforgiveness in their hearts. I know because I had unforgiveness in my heart "for over seventy years."

I am grateful to God the Holy Spirit led Linda to my bedside after leaving the "Purity Is Power" conference in Houston. He gave her specific instructions related to me dealing with a lot of unresolved issues from my past. Although I had eleven siblings, only God could make me free. Hearing and deliverance will make you free as well. One positive thing that came out of that area was the new L-shape school that was converted into a church. Now in that atmosphere, there's praise and worship music going forth, as opposed to memories of stolen innocence.

Safety tips

- Be aware of the company you keep
- Travel in pairs when going out
- Do not be afraid to speak out
  (This gets a lot of men in trouble)
- Speak up and do not be afraid to expose a predator

- Joe Bridgewater

Hospital Visit

It was Saturday, August 20th, 2016 at around 10.30 PM.

The doctor just left the room and said that I would be partially awake during my procedure. Out of obedience to the instructions of the Holy Spirit, my daughter showed up at my bedside. She shared with me the need to repeat a sinner's prayer and confession, which I did:

> I, Joe Bridgewater, make this confession to God. Lord God, forgive

me of my sins, the sin of comission and omission, any infidelity and misguided thoughts, any lustful way of thinking, any unclean or any ungodly spirits that have existed in me from the beginning of time…all the way through my bloodline, I renounce and rebuke that spirit off my bloodline in the name of Jesus, and I ask you to cleanse my heart, forgive me of my sins and make me right before you, in Jesus' name, I pray, Amen.

Then she began reading, "Proverbs 28:13 (NKJV) – He who covers his sins will not prosper, but whoever confesses and forsakes them will have mercy." Linda shared, I no longer conceal any sin that was in my life, in my bloodline from the beginning of time, even with my father, my grandfather, anyone in my bloodline. Most importantly, my violation was NOT my fault. It is time for you and me to rise up and walk. Forgive yourself and free your mind. Repeat the confession above and break any generational curse off your seed leading back to the beginning of time.

Your Charge

Now, all the men, women, grandchildren, great-grandchildren, great-great-grandchildren and on and on will prosper due to your confession to be free. Begin walking in the power and authority which God has given you as the paternal headship of your home. Speak life into every situation. Gain control over your household and impart it to the next generation. Speak life into your lineage and your descendants so everyone will prosper in heaven and on Earth. God can use a black sheep in your family to intercede on your behalf on the next generation. Sometimes you must adjust your prayer or target them more specifically for them to come to pass. When you come from generations of brokenness, there may not be a good example to mirror your relationship from, but if you keep your focus on the cross... God can, and He will set you free. You just have to make up in your mind that you are tired of living that type of life, and that you desire to be free.

Your traumatic experiences do not have a hold of you; they don't control you... unless you allow them to. You have the power and authority that God has given you to break everything off of you that has you bound. Mentally, we have generations of people; men, women, and children that need to be made free. They are still bound by something in their past or something in their life right now. Only you can make up in your mind to change that statistic. Society believes men do not want to get the help they need and it is time to prove them wrong. It is time to create a generation, a culture, of therapeutic men ready to do the work of the ministry, edify the Body of Christ, and uplift the Kingdom of God, in life, business, and career. We are more than conquerors through Christ Jesus, and it is time for us to exemplify that in "everything" we do.

Men are the headship. They must lead by example and be healed from past circumstances. It is to use what God has already given us to conquer the enemy. Those strategies, principles, and doctrines are revealed through His word. It is time to be made free. If you utilize the strategies illuminated in this book, compare them to your situation, the Spirit will reveal to you how you need to be made free. There are supernatural healing and forgiveness aligned in the chapters of this book. All you have to do is receive our stories of being an overcomer by the Blood of the Lamb and the words of our testimony. Look at it this way; if I, Joe Bridgewater, could embrace supernatural healing and forgiveness of the young boys that raped me, surely you can forgive someone that has wronged you. In Matthew 6:15 (NKJV) Jesus says, "But if you do not forgive men their trespasses, neither will your Father forgive your trespasses." You do not need to hear apologies from your offender, just forgive them. It is so freeing!

Get ready to be empowered by another overcomer by the name of Bruce Lee. Yes, his name really is Bruce Lee. His father was in the penitentiary, accused of murder but he overcame those circumstances later with the aid of his son, Bruce Lee. Unfortunately, he did not get an opportunity to appreciate that before dying in prison. What about you? Are you ready to use these personal development strategies presented in FREEDOM to shake off the trauma of your past and change your mindset?

Let's do a simple exercise toward creating a culture of therapeutic men. Take ten minutes to annotate what person, place, or experience still has you in mental bondage:

_____

_____

_____

_____

FREEDOM

UNBOUND:

Breaking the Chains

By Bruce Lee

My father and mother got divorced when I was five years old. My father was an alcoholic and very abusive to my mother. He was never around in my life. I wished I had a father figure that would take me camping, fishing, teach me about sports, and about manhood. Unfortunately, every time I saw him, he would be drunk and very abrasive toward my mother. So, I do not remember a lot about him as a young child. Fast forward into my teen years, my father was accused of murdering a young lady and sentenced to the penitentiary.

Although we did not really have a relationship, I still felt sad, hurt, and heart-broken at hearing the verdict. What young child wants to hear that his father has been sentenced to the penitentiary? What young man? I knew he was violent but did not think he was capable of killing anyone. I was in total disbelief about the whole matter. What happened was not a family secret. However, my entire family became silent about the issue. And, I really believe, if he did it, he was provoked in some sort of way.

Prison Life/Death

Life continued on as fifteen to twenty years passed. Out of the blue, my family received news that my father had become very ill while serving out his time. Now, here we go again. Another flood of emotions began to surface in me. Have you ever been torn between caring for someone and not caring for them? I wanted to stay upset at him for not being in my life, then on the other hand, I was concerned that he was sick. I could not imagine him being locked up and dying behind bars. Especially, after still feeling he was innocent of killing his landlord's crackhead daughter. His condition kept getting worse as the day passed by. Days became weeks and weeks became months. Without any notice, the unexpected happened. News came that he died from complications tied to diabetes. Diabetes?

I was on an emotional rollercoaster trying to understand everything. Now I am faced with his death as his namesake. A permanent reminder I would never see him again. This pain was too hard to bear! All these incidents put me into a mental prison of emotions: abandonment, rejection, embarrassment, murder, crackhead, prison, death, diabetes, and others. Oh Lord, what is next?

I do not even remember the day I decided to fight back and speak on his behalf. All I know, the pain was so unbearable. God raised up holy boldness in me and I became a voice to prove my father's innocence and clear his name. I hired some attorneys to get the murder charge dropped. And, we were successful, thank God.

Seeking Help

One of the biggest things I would like to get across regarding men is the importance of having a father in a child's life. There are certain responsibilities only a "father" can teach his son. Of course, we know this may not be true in every paternal relationship. We must start somewhere and help raise a culture of therapeutic men not ashamed to seek help or learn how to cope with different situations. Most definitely, it is a process and collaborative effort between our communities and men. See, I did not realize how messed up I was, lacking the presence of my father in my life. Do not get me wrong, I did see him…he left an impression…but it was a negative one. He was either drunk or violent with my mother.

Functioning Alcoholic

As a young African-American male that was not taught much in life, his presence had a reverse effect on me. I do not think he got any good life skills from my grandfather. Over the years, I heard a lot about my grandfather. And knowing of him, I never remembered him drinking. Not sure where my dad got the ability or influence of drinking. However, I do not believe he got that from his father or anyone else I know. But there has to be something to associate the behavior, trigger, or root causes with.

My grandfather was gentle and somewhat kindhearted. I remember being a young man on the farm with my sister, picking peas, watermelon, tomatoes, and all the other fruits and vegetables. So, with that being said, it is important to have a man, not only in a boy's life but in a child's life. It is very impactful. Especially after realizing that some of my adult issues stemmed from paternal emotional abandonment. Meaning, I wished and wanted a lot of things to happen that never did come to pass.

Loving Mentality?

At age eleven, I ended up getting my first job to help out in the home. My mother really was not there because she worked three jobs just to "keep a roof over our head, clothes on our back, and food to eat" for me and my two sisters. We were raised in a home to equate these basic parental responsibilities as "I love you."

Back then, love was, "Hey, I am feeding and clothing you." It was not really stated or shown. In that day and time, that was how they spelled love: "Me clothing you… feeding you, and putting a roof over your head." Not saying there was anything wrong with it. Simply, I do not remember being young and being told, "I love you." I think it is important as adults to tell our kids we love them. We have to hug them and shower them with unconditional love. We cannot just say, "Okay, well, I am feeding and clothing you."

We have to really sit down and talk to our kids and listen to our kids. Listen to what they are saying and what they are not saying. By now, I did not associate or acknowledge any pattern or root causes…but I did later. Nor did I realize everything that happened thus far paternally or maternally had in any measure traumatized me. No man ever wants to admit that. Fortunately, it is time for men to come out of that mindset and not continue to pass that behavior to the next generation.

FREEDOM

Role Model

I remember one time when my dad kind-of broke into our apartment. He was drunk and really abrasive. He jumped on my mother. He had a gun and his plan was to kill everybody in the house, which was traumatic for me and my family.

Growing up with two sisters and a mother, I really did not have a role model in the house but I always attended church and the church poured off into me. But that was pretty much on a Wednesday and Sunday. All the other days, I did not have that. I am not saying that it made me a bad person. However, it did really affect me. Just by doing this book, I really had an eye-opening experience. I did not even know that some of the things I was dealing with really affected me so deeply. There were areas from my past I thought I was "over" ...but the residue surfaced. Learn to deal with your residue before it deals with you.

One major reason my father was not in my life was, I do not think he really knew "how to be a father." He always worked. Men tend to hide behind work. He was a functioning alcoholic. He would always work and after work, he would drink or go to different bars and clubs, hang out, and be with different women. So that being said, I think that really paid a toll on me and my sister's life. I have one older and one younger sister.

Latchkey Influencers

We lived in an apartment when we were younger and moved into a house. After our parents separated, we pretty much moved from apartment complex to another. That also paid a toll on us. There were not really any rules in the house. We pretty much stayed inside the house and did not have a childhood experience, a lot of friends, or just hanging out. I was too sheltered from life experiences around me, we were latchkey kids.

I remember being around a childhood friend that drank. As I entered high school, I found myself drinking with him. Before I realized it, I was becoming an alcoholic like my father. I had to really be mindful and start thinking about how to plan because I did not want to be like him. I did not want to do the things he did, I wanted and had to make some changes. Yes, alcohol was easily accessible in high school. And yes, I would leave school and go to the liquor store and purchase the alcohol. I would come back to school and still do my work. This also paid a toll on me because I saw my dad do the "same thing." I still did not acknowledge any pattern of root causes tied to my dad.

In reminiscing, I remember riding with him to East Texas, one of the things he would give me was a beer. I mean, before I was ten years old, I was drinking a beer with my dad. No fishing. No camping…just drinking beer. Our time together mainly consisted of something that was pretty much on the negative side.

Latchkey Kids

A child who is at home without adult supervision for some part of the day, especially after school until a parent returns from work. At times, they have keys to their home hanging from their neck.

– Wiikpedia.org

My Heart's Desire

I thank God that I am still here. He has allowed me another chance to get it right. Now, I am not trying to bash my father. I thank God for my father and mother. If it were not for them, God putting them together, I would not be the man I am today. Of course, I wanted some things to be a little different. I would have wanted him to play a major part in my life and hang out together, even if my mother and father were not together. I would have wanted them to say, "Okay, go out and play catch… go to the park." Or he could have taught me about different sports, took me fishing, camping, or just have a heart-to-heart talk. You know, that rite of passage stuff. That interaction is what I think men lack in building a healthy relationship with their sons. The lack of this played a major role in my life and added to any insecurities I hid in plain sight.

Reality Check

I did not realize back then I was traumatized by the actions of my father and forcefulness of my mother. All I knew how to do was work. No one taught me the different facts of life, how to balance things, or even how to balance a checkbook. I just knew that I would get a job and be able to buy different things. Now, how to balance life, it was not shown, and it really was not taught in school. I cannot stress the importance of children needing to be taught to balance life and life skills. They should also have book knowledge. That is where both parents play a major part in a person's life.

I mentioned earlier my father was accused of murder and he went to a penitentiary. He was accused of murdering his landlord's daughter, who was hooked on drugs. She and her boyfriend broke into my father's home and demanded some money. Her boyfriend left but she stayed behind. My father ended up killing the young lady and left her abandoned in the house till he put cardboard over the body. But it was pretty much an act of self-defense. At the time of the incident, nobody had any money for a lawyer and I think I was living out of the States. As minorities, we did not need to settle for a plea, we needed to get a lawyer and plead our case in court.

Diabetes: Silent Killer

My father went to the penitentiary where at the time, he was diagnosed with diabetes. Diabetes and penitentiary life did not work together because he was not taking care of himself. He started losing limbs. Both of his legs were amputated. Next thing we knew, he ended up passing away. I did not know how to feel, let alone, grieve during this time in my life. However, I am still grateful to God for the opportunity I was given to speak at his funeral.

One of the things confirmed during this period was my father's salvation. Prior to his death, he committed his life to Christ. I was happy just to know that and I felt comfortable knowing that. Even after all the things he did, he rededicate his life back to Christ; I believe his soul is resting in heaven.

A Mother Cannot Be a Father

Now with that being said, I had a little money. I did not want the lasting memory of my father to be a "murderer that died in a penitentiary." So, I pursued his case to clear his name. Against many odds, I was able to spend quite a bit of money to get his name cleared. That was a major accomplishment I am most proud of. Most definitely, if I had to do things over again, my desire would be for my parents to be together, my father to be a better father to me, be able to sit down for a father-son talk, be able to ask him questions, be able to talk about some things that were going on in my childhood or at school, and talk about some things going on with a female.

My father, not being consistently in my life, affected every relationship I had with females. As I got older, I came to the realization that my mother could never replace my father. While previously, I compensated for

FREEDOM

that void in my life by giving my mother a Father's Day card. The reality finally set in that my mother could "never" ever replace my father. So, I stopped giving her Father's Day card. She will always be my mother, but she could never replace nor be my father. The pieces of the puzzle were starting to make some sense.

Now, I love my mother to life. I love my father to life. Thank God for both of them because without them, I would not be here. I am deeply indebted to both of them. And as I move further in my career and in my life, I am committed to constantly talking to my daughter. As we get a little further, I will discuss my son. Not only that, but I am also able to speak life into many children as much as possible. When I go to a conference or somewhere else, I let them know how important it is to be in their kid's life. Not that the father has to be with the mother of your child, but it is important to be around for the kids; sitting around, talking to them, letting them know that you love them, and that they mean so much to you. I do not recall or remember even having my father say that, not in a sober moment. Everything he said was always behind a lot of alcohol and beer. As a matter of fact, I do not recall him even telling me he loved me. He might have, I just do not remember. So, I continued to pray and press on.

CREATING A THERAPEUTIC CULTURE OF MEN

My suggestion to divorced or separated couples would be to remain in communication with their child and look for the good in them. That is one thing adults seem to lack in understanding; how their decisions affect the child. Children can be traumatized. I told you before, I did not realize it at the time. But my sisters and I were traumatized as kids and "never got any type of counseling," we carried everything into adulthood. Now we wonder why we are having relationship issues in our adult life. Especially, where there was no stability fostered from our parents' relationship.

I love my mother for working three jobs and providing our needs. She was only doing what she knew in the absence of my father. However, she tried to play both roles, which she could not do. Now, I understand how life is and how society has changed. Actually, both parents need to be in their kids' life and not one pretending to be both parents. That was how God designed everything when He created Adam and Eve. He created the man, took his rib and created Eve to establish a union. That is not saying that we have to always agree. It is fine to agree to disagree for the sake of the kids.

This strategy is one I share with families daily when discussing my absentee father, or other relatives like my father's brothers. They were not great fathers either.

Are you starting to recognize a pattern? You may not have the assets or everything you desire. You may not have been taught everything you think you should. That is where the Bible plays the major part in our lives and the Holy Spirit teaches us. Never forget there are great self-help books to help us along our journey.

Speak Life

It is important that we continually press on and be vigilant about the kids' mindset. If I had to do it over again, not saying I do not know how to fish, but I would want to be taught by my father. I would want him to show me different sports. I would want to walk and talk about things that have transpired in my life. I know I cannot rewind it. So now, I have to look at the present. Currently, I want to be as prevalent as possible in many kids' lives. Not just boys but girls because it is important for fathers to be in their kids' lives, to bring life to it, to let them know how important they are and how valuable they are. I do not recall my father telling me I was important or I was valuable.

As I got older, I heard it more from my mother. But when I was younger, the only thing I remember was, "Hey, I am showing you I love you by me going to work every day... you eating and me putting a roof over your head... I am feeding and clothing you." However, I know kids need more. It is so important that we understand that. I pray that this book may be able to help some people out. It is helping me. It is letting me know half the things that were lying dormant, which I pray to The Father to cast out that it may leave me, or that He may take it all away. Although God had me covered, my prayer still included not allowing me to turn out like my father or end up in jail. I do not want to go to jail. I try to make sure that I do not have any tickets, and I present myself as an outstanding citizen.

Other Women

I was talking about my father not being in my life and how it affected me. I did not realize how bad it affected me and other relationships I was involved in over the years. I did not know how to communicate because I really did not have anyone to confide in or sit down and talk to. It really drew a wedge in me and I was always withdrawn. I happened to be in a relationship with a woman when these events took place. Saying my relationship with her was affected is an understatement. It was not easy trying to find someone that loved me for me, even when I did not love myself.

FREEDOM

My insecurities of not loving myself were tied to my absentee father. Like I said, I did not realize "how much" it affected me until I was in a relationship with a woman. I really did not know how to hold a conversation with a woman, sit down and talk, or how to be real with her after seeing my father with different women. Just like other men in society, I operated according to what I knew. It was "normal" for a man to be with as many women as he could be…. I was no different.

As you see, now I am getting my training from other influences. Mainly because, I did not get proper training of manhood, boyhood, the different stages of life relating to women, how to challenge different things, how to be able to respond to women, or simply, just talk to my own daughter. At the time, I did not have a good relationship with her mother and that drew a wedge between my daughter and me.

Time for another simple exercise. Annotate any issue you are having communicating with your child's mother or another person:

_____

_____

_____

_____

_____

_____

Further instructions will be given at the end of the book.

_____

As of today, my daughter and I are good friends. We text and talk almost every day, but it has not always been that way because I did not know "how" to be a good communicator, did not know how to be the father, the husband, the friend, or just to be able to sit down and hold a conversation. I think it plays a major part for us men. There is good news! You still have time to learn how to be a good communicator.

Parental Challenge

One of the things I talk to parents about and challenge them to do with their kids is to sit down for 45 minutes a day with them and ask them how their day went. Then, actively listen to their response. I never had a chance to do this or I never recall doing this with my mother since she worked three jobs... she was never there. Then, with my parents' divorce when I was five years old...he was never there. And he stayed right in the same city. His idea of spending time around me consisted of indulging in alcohol, going to clubs while I would sit in the car waiting for him to do what he did in the club, watch him drive home drunk or whatever it might be. So, I did not have the experience of really communicating with him. The lack of this skill affected me most of my life. But it does not have to be that way with you and your kids. You can make the necessary adjustments now that will change the rest of your life.

Now, I know a man is probably the priest, provider and protector of the home. However, I did not know that back then. I thank God where I am now... it took me some time to get here. As being a priest, provider, and protector doesn't mean that --- It is a process because it is not about the man paying all the bills, it could be the woman paying the bills. She could have a better job. Whatever the case may be, you want to be able to communicate. This is what my wife and I are working on right now. I pray to God that He works with me and through me so I will be able to tap into different things. I want to be able to indulge, communicate, and talk with my daughter about our grand-daughters.

I want our grand-daughters to have it a lot better than what I experienced. Surely, I want my daughter to have a better relationship with her husband. Yes, it takes some communication, and it is a process. Most importantly, that process has to begin somewhere. It is so important as a group of people, body of believers, that we embrace this process. When I put God first in my life, He revealed why my past relationships did not work out.

As I worked on this book with my wife and my father-in-law, I understood that there were some things still lying at my doorstep that I thought I was over or I did not realize it still affected me. My prayer is that I will continue to press on while becoming a better communicator in all my relationships. So, let me encourage and challenge you to keep pressing to become a better communicator. Do not allow your past circumstances to define your present situation. Do not continue to blame others, simply learn from the experience, and make the necessary life-changes to receive any help you may need.

FREEDOM

Guilt and Shame

As of today, I communicate with my mother on a day-to-day basis. I am always trying to flip negative things into something positive. Not saying that I always agree with what my mother says or does. I am simply stating that I respect her as my mother and I continue to pray for her and with her. I always felt guilty because of my father not being there. Back in those days, during my military years, I always sent my checks home. My father was not paying child support for my siblings and I wanted to make sure I did my part to help. I felt "guilty" and really wanted to support my mother during that time. I am not saying this was good or bad. However, I was doing only what I had been taught to do since age eleven.

Whereas now, sometimes I still feel guilty about my decisions as a result of my childhood. I know that my first responsibility is to my wife and our home. And of course, I give to our kids when my wife and I are in agreement or when possible. If I have something left over, I would then be able to help and assist my mother. But even when I was in the military, I would send money home to assist and help out in hopes of setting up a saving account. Unfortunately, I was not shown or trained how to manage finances for different things. Today, I am blessed to say that my communication and relationships are getting better. And I am learning how to manage my finances. I can no longer blame my parents for what I did not learn. Neither can you. I must proceed on from here knowing I did not get here overnight and this behavior will not change overnight. Continue to ask the Father for guidance, wisdom, and understanding of what we are supposed to be doing. He left us the Holy Spirit to help us.

Prayer Changes Things

One of my favorite prayers is for God to give me some understanding. I want to have some clarity about what I am trying to do, what I want to be or what I want to establish. I no longer want to be affected by my past relationships, past things that transpired with other women; my daughter and I had a rough relationship because of the things that transpired between me her mother and me. But thank God, we have continued to work on that. Likewise, I am working on my relationship with my wife. My advice to you would be to develop a prayer life or deeper prayer life. Let God mend your relationships as He reveals more about yourself. Unlike my father, I never was abusive in my relationships. I always wanted to walk out or just leave. I did not want to face it head-on, the way I should have - sit down and communicate it or sit down and just listen. I was still mimicking the way I saw my father handle situations. My prayer is for God to remove that from my life. Although, I am better than I was in days back, thank God, I still have work to do.

I am going to continue to stay in God's word, get self-help books, get into relationship conferences; I will continue doing all that to help me become a better individual, better man, better husband, and a better father. I saw my father make enough mistakes with our family; drinking alcohol, and chasing women. That curse stops here....no more dysfunctional behavior! Now I acknowledge any pattern of root causes was tied to me mimicking my father. I know it is a process for me, on a day-to-day basis, to really work on myself so I can become a better father, a better husband, a better grandfather because of the blessings from God, knowing that He is my number one source. He is who I need to believe in and He is who I put my trust in.

Be careful how you represent yourself just because you are not with the child's mother or whomever we want. Whoever is your child's mother, it does not mean that you should act up and not show attention to your children. We sure want to train and show them along the way how to be more effective role models. My thing is, just because I was not shown how to be a good role model does not mean I can continue use that as an excuse in life. You cannot either. My assignment now is to help other people that need to be free. We need a therapeutic culture of men ready to pour into the next generation. Book signing and conferences are just a small avenue to reach other people. You must have a consistent prayer life and let God be God.

We want to continue to grow, breathe life into others, and breathe life into our own lives. You cannot change the past, now I look at it and say, "Okay, I have got to position myself to be better. I have got to position myself for my future to be better." So how can I be better in my today and in my future? Prayer. The answer was right in front of me. It is important that we continue to pray, press and be positive about the things that we do. We never know whom we can affect. We never know when somebody is looking at us because there are people that are continually looking at us; people who mimic what we do. I know that I would not want to do anything to make my daughter or my grandkids look bad. I know that they are going to be looking up to their G-papa. I do not want to hurt them.

Here I am, being a role model, being a father, being a husband, being a grandfather, being an uncle to a lot of kids that do not have that major role model. I watch what I say, watch how I say it. I watch what I do; mindful that I am being watched. Somebody is looking up to me to see if I am going to resort to being like my daddy. I can remember some things that transpired. There were some who said, "You are going to be like your daddy. You are going to be nothing." But I refused to believe that. I am positive. I am praying. I am pressing because I am going to be more than what my daddy showed me. I am not being negative, I love my daddy to life. I said a prayer for him to change his mindset and dedicate his life back to Christ. I thank God he did. I thank God for my life; He has allowed me to pursue some things and to go even higher and higher.

It is important, as a body of believers, that we continue to be a focal point in people's lives. Meaning; how can we look at and do something that is totally different? How can we be positive and not ruin lives? In my situation, it did ruin some relationships. It messed up some things with my daughter. But your results can be different when you implement the strategies presented in this book.

A Father's Rights

By now, you are familiar with my past relationship with other family members. Please bear with me as I share memories of my son, my past, and some more history. Of course, I talked about relationships and things that transpired with my mother and other females, it was not that great. Well, my son is not in my life due to some other trauma from another failed relationship.

I had morals and beliefs about marriage, finding a good wife, and having kids to help along the way. It did not happen the way I wanted. However, I was able to have a son and he is not in my life but I continue to support him financially. I would love to be more supportive by being in his life because my father was not in my life and I wanted to do something different. Lo and behold, that is not because of anything that I have done or caused. It is just that it did not work out.

His mother has done a lot of traveling all over the country. She has moved to several different states. It has been really difficult to just to find out where they are exactly. I have hired investigators, lawyers, and paid so much money to be a major part in my son's life. It has not turned out the way I like. Even at one point, I stopped paying child support to see if my son and his mother would surface. Lo and behold, nothing ever happened. One thing that surprised me, however, was being threatened to pay child support or I would have to go to jail. So of course, I did not want to do any jail time

FREEDOM

so I turned everything over to my lawyer at that time. His comment was that I needed to start back paying. And my thoughts were, "Why do I have this lawyer?" I am sure any person with a similar experience can relate to my feelings.

So even till this day, I am still praying that one day I will be able to see my son and sit down and have some long talks with him. For a while, I was writing one letter a week to him when I had an address to send it to. I am always in contact with his other grandmother and grandfather, just to see how they are doing. It is unfortunate, but they have not seen or heard from their daughter or the other grandkids in a long time. All we can do is pray for my son and his mother. Like I said, she has a couple of other kids from her marriage after me. I pray that they are all okay. I think it is so important to be in the kids' life and that is what I love doing to other kids around me. I just love them and help as many people as possible.

Some years ago, missing my son devastated me to a point where I went into a little depression. It was kind of hard on me! My way of dealing with it was to move to another state just to try to get my focus back on me. Establishing order in my life was one of my priorities along with trying to be there for my daughter. Shortly after, I went into depression mode. By no means did I know what anxiety was, let alone how to take care of it.

I was functioning in a way but then, I was not functioning. I was not social. I was not really going out and doing what normal people did. I would maybe go to church every now and then and then I would return home. It got to a point where I started acting like my father by drinking. When I went to bed, something I depended on was a bottle... having a bottle every day. I became a functioning alcoholic but I did not call it that at that time. But I am calling it now. I thank God for a praying mother and grandmother.

My grandmother's no longer alive but we always talked pretty much on a day-to-day basis. She knew what was going on with me. Her advice was to continue to press on, pray, and not to give up. I thank God I remembered and I did not give up. So, I got off my pity-party and continued to press on. I went to different colleges, have a few different degrees and some certificates. I am a Certified Trauma-Informed Care Specialist, some call me a practitioner. Part of my daily responsibilities involves doing a lot of speaking engagements with kids and parents regarding trauma. How ironic, in revisiting my past for this book, it really brought up some old residue and some things I had thought were over. And, as I

FREEDOM

think back, I cannot help but pray for my son. As I stated, I have got a great relationship with my daughter, but my continuous prayer is to be reunited with my son.

Advice I share with families today: it is so important that even though relationships or marriages may not work out but you want them to continue, unless that person is doing something detrimental, you always want to be able to have a working relationship with your mate or significant other that they can be in their kids' life. Not only the sons need their fathers, the girls also need their father. We need to be reminded of that on a regular basis.

So, I thank God for having so much love for me and unconditional love that I can continue to pray and press on, even about some things that did not work out in my favor as I thought they should. Like having my son in my life because I wanted to be the one to coach my son in football, basketball, baseball, and not only just sports but also going with him to the library… doing some readings. These are some of the things that I do with my nephew when I spend time with him because I know his father is not in his life.

Revelation

One of the things that I love to tell parents is; "You do not want to overcompensate because somebody is not in their life. You would want to be able to sit down and talk to them. Secondly, there are repercussions to our actions. So, when a person messes up, it is important that there are some consequences that are attached to it." So, it is important that he asks, "Did I learn any lesson from this experience?" Believe me, I want to do something different. That was my mindset in every relationship I was in; I wanted to do something different. But not knowing, I still was hurt, I was still traumatized yet functioning. I will talk about that in the next segment. It was nothing for me to sink deeper in depression and I did not even understand what was going with me. In my mind, I thought I was fine. But the reality was that I actually needed some help and God gives us provisions to seek godly counsel or free will to seek counselors and therapists. I had to seek some counseling at one point in my life. Of course, a lot of people try to stereotype those actions. I just really needed to get some things off my chest in order to regain some balance in my life and be mentally free.

FREEDOM

Regaining Balance

Desperately, I was trying to return to normality. I had a routine that included a well-balanced meal, together with taking my vitamins. And today, I still do that. As I pray, not only do I pray, not only do I fast and pray but I also seek some type of help and there is nothing wrong. I know that men have that pride thing going on, but that is where things are tied to. I not only had commitment issues but I had issues with not knowing that I had commitment issues. I thought I was okay and a lot of times, we do think that we are okay and not knowing that we need a lot of purging. And as you elevate, then there are some other things that may pop-up that you will not understand.

It is just like me writing this book. I had thought all the time that I was OK, but I was not. My wife discerned things from a totally different perspective and said I was not fine emotionally. Also, there was a point in my life where I did not know I was a people-pleaser, instead of God-pleaser. I guess I wanted to have good friends. Today, I just thank God for where I am right now.

Of course, I want to help people and that is what I am. Most importantly, I want to make sure I put God first in my life. It is important that I continue to press and pray and acknowledge my father. I think it is important for me to assist people along the way because there is somebody out there that has gone through something similar or maybe the same thing that I have gone through. I may be able to assist him because men have that pride thing with them. We do not like to say, "Okay, I need some help." But I am here to tell you, God has put people in your life to help you, coach you, assist you, and mentor you, to the next level. And as you get to the next level, there would possibly be somebody else in line.

So, I always try to grow knowing I am not a perfect person. I make efforts to learn as much as possible. Every day, I make my moves count. I have got to be mindful of what I say and what I do because I want to be transparent.

I have not always been this way. There was a time when I used to be very angry without knowing why I was angry. The revelation of identifying past hurts has been freeing. Even having to go and forgive my mother and father led to some healing, before and after the fact. Truly, it has been a trying time for me. But I am grateful to God for covering me over fifty years, every hour, every minute of my life. I know how important it is to continue to breathe life, continue to be a mouthpiece for people. It is important because people do not always get what they need. It is so important that I am here to help, not for any financial gain. You do not know how important it is to be mindful of the word and how important it is to study the word. As people point toward me, I point up in the air to my Father. Sharing my overcomer's story, I want to be able to bless somebody with some information that they can say, "Hey, man, I can use these tools. I can use this information."

Got My Swag Back

Now I can press on, here it is. Yes, my father was not in my life and my mother, as I got older, has been there though she had to work three jobs earlier. Nothing against her, nothing against my father. I had two sisters, they were very chatty at times. There was a point where I would get angry all the time because I did not get a chance to speak. As a result, I was always the quiet one. I did not laugh much.

As a matter of fact, my laugh was a quiet laugh. Now I am so much relieved and so much better; I laugh out loud and I smile now. I have some swag in my walk. I hold my head up. Like I said, I know who I am, I know whom I believe in, and I know who my Father is. I thank God for that. I thank God for the test that I have been through. If I had to do it over again, yes, I would do something totally different because I would want my son in my life. Breathing life into him would have been a pleasure. Training and teaching him would have been an honor. And what I do for my grandkids; I constantly call and talk to my grandkids and let them know how important and valuable they are. This is something we must do. We have to let them know how valuable and how important they are. In understanding how valuable I am, this book has helped me share my story. I thank God for blessing me and making me a better person, a better man, "Lord, I thank you. Lord, I love you. If it was not for you, planting that seed in, who would it have been?"

Coping Mechanism

Over forty years ago they called it trauma, but society's stigma on the word hinders many from getting help. One of the things they used to say back in those days was, "Boy, you are going to be all right... You are going to get over it... Just keep moving... Whatever happens, you are going to be all right."

I am here to tell people that if they do not seek any type

FREEDOM

of help or any type of assistance, it is going to be difficult to get over it. Yes, you may think that you are over it. Fortunately, something can easily trigger it to surface and come back up to your memory. That happened to me while working on this the book. My wife had been on me about meeting my deadlines for writing this book. In working on it, I had many epiphany moments that I had to pray my way through. A couple of my friends became a listening ear as I kept pressing through. I teach others sometimes with trauma, people's reactions are in three ways known as 3Fs: fight, flight or freeze...coping mechanisms.

A fight does not mean a physical fight. It could just be arguing. Flight means to run away (that used to be me) - run away from different situations. I did not meet situations head-on. I just ran. I was having issues because I did not know how to deal with things, so of course, I would run away. Freeze, yes, I would freeze a lot and shut down. Now I thank God that I am getting better with that.

I am working on my communication skills and it is a process, it is a day-to-day process of communicating. It is a day-to-day process because I am a trauma informed-care practitioner. That is my job. It is something I do almost seven days a week and as I teach it to people, it helps me out in a day-to-day process. I know it is about breaking chains and as I look at my life and I think things over, I thank God because I am here. A lot of the people would not be able to go through the things that I have gone through in my life. We stayed with different people over and over, different folks but I was able to maintain and was working on a job. I did not have much of a life because I began working at an early age.

I remember a lot about my age so I can get a newspaper route. I had a paper route. My paper route started as a walking paper route. Eventually, I was able to save up money to get myself a little-used bicycle. I had to pay somebody to help me because it turned out to be a major route. I paid them to drive me around and help me throw newspapers. Back then it was difficult, especially as a kid. Even in my teenage years, trying to collect money for the newspapers was difficult because people were always getting over on me. That was another traumatic experience because I always had "issues" when I recognized the same behavior.

Then I would go into a "flight" mood and I would just not deal with it and walk away. I would "walk away" from jobs, different situations, and different relationships. I would just shut down. I would "automatically" not finish things, I would run away. I

FREEDOM

have had nice jobs, situations may pop-up, or a relationship may not work out. I would "leave" a good paying job, screw up some things, "leave" from issues with family members, and I would "leave" not knowing that there was some traumatic experience that happened in my past. I was unable at the time, not knowing, how to deal with it. Does this sound like you when you respond to different situations?

Now I am at a point where I can speak and talk about different situations, meet different situations head-on. It is still a work in progress with me and so let me tell you guys, "Don't be afraid!" It is not about the 3Fs. It is about having a dialogue and communicating where: "This is how I am feeling now. This is what is going on with me." I think I did not even understand then that I had an anger problem. I did not realize I was dealing with an anger issue because of so much other stuff that was inside of me that was just closed in, just suppressed.

I thank God that He is working with me and through me on how to deal with different situations. I am still working on some things on a constant basis because I know that prayer changes all things. Now, here I am where I can assist and enlighten other people on becoming an overcomer. Part of that process was realizing it is okay to sit down and talk about "it" because God does give us provisions. Provisions sometimes are therapists, psychiatrists, and in the black community, we shun them. We are like, "Okay, boy, you are going to be all right... Let's pray... It is all in your head." But it takes a little bit more than that. It is important that we understand how important we are to get some things done so we can move, move, and move on in our life.

Even to this day, I thank God that He is working with me and through me because I have been a gentle giant at times. I know people see things in me that I may not see or they may have some suggestions that you may need to do this or that. My thing is, "I love to pray on it and see where God is taking me. I cannot go with somebody else's opinion." It is important, as a body of believers, that we look at that and remember how powerful we are and what we are supposed to do as a body of believers. I have to continue to be mindful because I understand that my trauma did not happen overnight and it will not get fixed overnight. Too many things surfaced that had been lying dormant.

Of course, I know of some great counselors and a couple of good psychiatrists that I can also talk with. But, it is really important that we ask people for help or call them. Do not be shy or run away from what is going on in your life. With that being said, it is so important that we are a testament for other people. Our lifestyle should make us become a mouth-piece for God. Then, others might not be scared to seek any help, especially with men because we have that pride where we do not like to discuss certain things nor share them. Each time I drank alcohol, I would be smiling all the time, would be cool, calm, collected, and not violent. But I thank God, He delivered me from that but I am still a work in progress.

I want to be able to help out as many people as possible, not just men but women also. I am going to let the women know that they do not want to push a man where he shuts down, acts out, or runs away. You would want to meet him where he is and accept him for what he has to offer.

If you had trauma as a child and did not get treated as a child, it would affect your adult life. That was what happened to me, it affected my adult life; I did not even know that I was traumatized, that I had some issues, that I had depression, anxiety, anger and that I was shutting down. And it was because of the things that happened to me in my life. So, it is so important that we look at how we communicate with one another and make sure that we find a person that we can confide in, so we can share some things that are going on with us. Furthermore, we also have to look for a mentor or a life coach who will be able to work some things out with us.

Self-Care Is Critical

So, it is important because you look at the world and 92% of our society have had some type of traumatic experience. But it is what we do afterward, what type of help we seek, and what type of self-help and self-care we engage in that matter. We can all give great advice but if you have got some things that are lying dormant and maybe you are aware of them or you are not aware of them, you do not do yourself justice.

You want to be able to take care of yourself and you want to be able to make sure that you can recognize some things which might have happened in your life, and/or are still happening in your life and how you can overcome them. Ask yourself; "How can I break the chain? And how can I withstand this anxiety, this depression, and this thing that is a generational curse? How can I break it?"

It starts by getting into the scriptures, the word of God, praying and then also finding someone that can be your counselor, psychiatrist, or therapist whom you can confide in.

Get yourself a well-balanced meal, drink enough water and also make sure that you have got a good multi-vitamin. I am not really for medicines but I know that some people do need medicines to self-regulate themselves but water is one of the best things to self-regulate yourself with.

Look at some breathing techniques. How can I work on breathing better? Even getting something as simple as bubblegum or double bubble helps soothe my mind and body. I want to be able to live over one hundred years old. In doing so, it means I will have to look and do some self-care now. Your self-help or self-care may be different from mine. If I need to go to a doctor, need to see a counselor or a psychiatrist, I need to make that move. It is so important to get the help you need because you do not have all the answers.

I can give great advice but then I will also need to look at taking some advice. People do a lot of speaking engagements, give out a lot of advice but do they take their own advice?

So, I want to be the one -- I want to be a living example.

Not only do I want to breathe life into you but I want to breathe life into myself. I have to be mindful of some root causes and make sure that their triggers do not break me. I am letting loose, I am letting go of some things. What about you?

By doing that, I am reminded of how powerful God is and how He set some things in place for me. It is important that we are reminded of that daily. It does not build in a day. It is a process. I want to really get myself equipped when I go to any training in school; what can I do? What can I say? How can I go to these seminars, summits, conferences to learn more? As I learn more, I keep working on myself so that I can help others also.

In summary, this is my way of blessing everybody on how I overcame my trauma. It is a daily process. Remember, in the beginning, I didn't know what I was experiencing was called trauma. I was just told that I needed to "get over it." We need to STOP saying that in the minority community because you cannot just "get over stuff." It is a process.

FREEDOM

Call to Action

It is important to look deep down inside of yourself and try to see what you can do to seek some help and do some self-care. Look at maybe getting a counselor, mentor, or life coach. Seek some advice. Like I said, I am not a proponent for medicine, but well-balanced meals, multi-vitamins are good, and just talking about it. Do not allow pride to be the reason you do not seek any help, as opposed to holding things in.

Also, we always like to try to change things. We think that we can figure things out and I will be honest with you, God did not make us that way. He has somebody assigned to us and we have to take advantage of it and use that to the best of our abilities. Meaning yes, we need to pray, we need to fast and we need to go deep into the scripture and get into the word.

God allows us provisions that we may get some type of personal help to assist us, especially when we have trauma. If you do not get any type of help when you are dealing with trauma, it can be detrimental. It can really not only harm you but it can also harm others and I know that no one wants to harm their kids or harm their mate or even harm other people. It is important that you seek some help. Go deep within, try to get some advice and see what you can do to get it. Like I said, do some good soul searching.

What can I do to make a positive change in my life? How can I look at it? It is all about --- **S.M.A.R.T Goals.**

>S.M.A.R.T Goals – goals should be clear, concise, and obtainable:
>
>- Specific
>- Measurable
>- Attainable
>- Realistic
>- Timely

Put a timetable on your goal. You do not want to continue to be going around suffering in silence, as I call it sometimes. This helps eliminate the desire for the 3Fs: Fight, Flight or Freeze mode.

I know, as men, we have that tendency for the 3Fs or we possess great pride. Thus, we often do not want to console or confide in anybody, especially if it is a woman. But there is nothing wrong with confiding in someone, being upfront, honest, and telling people you are suffering because it can help.

FREEDOM

My story is that I want to be able to help other folks. And just by telling a part of my story, if it can help one person, I have done some good. I pray that this small book helps multiple people. I want to be open and upfront, where we can share some things and hopefully, we can break some cycles, break some curses, be free from that bondage and as we get free from that bondage and as we are helping other folks, you will also want to be able to help yourself.

It is important that we look at how and what we can do differently based on what transpired in our past. Never allow the events from your past to define you. Learn and grow from them. Most importantly, heal and be made free from those experiences using the strategies in this book:

- Associate triggers with suppressed memories
- Acknowledge any pattern of root causes
- Embrace supernatural healing and forgiveness
- 5 Keys to Forgiveness
- Make an open confession to heal
- 7 Stages of Emotional Adjustment

With that being said, I keep working on myself, trying to build up, be the man that the God has deemed for me to be. Not only be the man but I want to be able to enlighten other people when I share my story. Truly, my test has been my testimony. We believe this book, book signing or conferences will provide wisdom, knowledge and some great advice. I do not have all the answers, but being free from bondage is an awesome thing because nobody wants to be in bondage. And sometimes, we do not even know we are in bondage. We just go in through the motions.

So that is one of the things that trauma does to you; you can still be functioning and not even realize that you have some issues, have some things that need to be worked on, have some things that need to be prayed over, need to seek some counseling, and seek some advice.

It is important that as men, we do that to the utmost so that we can strive to be better leaders. Men are supposed to be the head and we need to take our rightful spot in society. I want to take my rightful spot and not only be the priest, provider, and protector of my home. But, be able to share what I have with others so that even if they go through some of the things that I have grown from they may not falter.

There is an enjoyment in helping others. I want to be able to help the young, the old and not just men but women also. Women also have a tendency of holding a lot of things in. Trauma does not only affect men, it also affects women.

FREEDOM

Take a self-examination and ask, "'Hey, I want to be free from bondage? How can I be free from bondage?" My suggestion is, if you want to be free from bondage, you have got to look at, "How can I get that way?" We all need to be able to be free to hear the chains breaking. We need to break those chains and be the men God has deemed us to be… the head and not the tail. So it is important that we look at being free from bondage, being trauma-free and making sure that relationships and communication happen. It starts by admitting that there is something going on and something that I need to work on.

There are some steps that we all have to take to get free from bondage. First of all, admit that you have some issues; there are some things you need to recover from. Next, with prayer, fasting, and the scripture, you can transform your mindset. Lastly, find a good Bible-based Church with some great teachings, a good covering, find a good mentor, a good life-coach; somebody that can be positive and speak positive things in your life. I know at times, people have the tendency to say the first thing that comes to their mind. I always tell folks, "You need to do the S.T.E.P. Method. You need to start, think, evaluate, pray, process and then proceed before letting something slip out of your tongue."

I will continue to pray and press on, believing that God and the Holy Ghost will propel you into FREEDOM! Thank you, thank you, thank you and God bless.

7 Stages of Emotional Adjustment

These are for every person going through crisis or any kind of progress through the stages of emotional adjustment. A victim may spend a great deal of time at one stage and only touch lightly on another or may pass through a number of stages over and over again, each time experiencing them in a different intensity. Furthermore, anyone close to the victim may experience these stages as well.

Number 1: Shock………………………………………………….. "I am numb."

Offering information to the victim during this stage is not helpful, as he or she will most likely remember very little, if anything, about what occurs during this time.

Number 2: Denial ………………………… "This couldn't have happened."

Not yet able to face the severity of the crisis, the victim spends time during this stage gathering strength. The period of denials serves as a cushion for the more difficult stages of adjustment which will follow.

FREEDOM

Number 3: Anger ……………………………… "What did I do? Why me?"

Much of the anger may be a result of the victim's feeling of loss of strength and loss of control over his or her own life. The anger may be directed toward the rapist, the doctor, the police or anyone else, including him or herself.

Number 4: Bargaining ………….. "Let's go on as if it didn't happen."

The victim sets up a bargain. He or she will not talk about the rape in exchange for not having to continue to experience the pain. In doing so, he or she continues to deny the emotional impact of rape. The impact the rape has had upon his or her life.

Number 5: Depression…………………."I feel so dirty, so worthless."

If the victim is warned of the stage ahead of time, he or she may not be so thrown by it. They may experience dramatic changes in sleeping or eating habits, indulging in compulsive rituals, or generalized fears completely taking over their lives. Professional counseling may be advisable. Though this is a painful time in their life, this stage shows they have begun to face the reality of the rape or whatever trauma they have. As they allow the negative emotions to surface, they should be reminded that these feelings are normal and will not last forever.

Number 6: Acceptance .... "Life goes on."

When enough of the anger and depression are released, the victim enters the stage of acceptance. They may still spend time thinking about the ugly experience, talking about the rape, for instance, but they understand and are in control of their own emotions and can now accept what happened to them.

Number 7: Assimilation .... "It's part of my life."

By the time the victim reaches this stage, they have realized their own self-worth and strength. They no longer need to spend time dealing with the rape or whatever trauma, as the total rape experience now mashes other experiences in their lives.[3]

---

[3] Adapted from Raped, by Deborah Roberts. Zondervan Publishing House, 1981. P. 157-159.

FREEDOM

FORGIVENESS

Forgiveness involves five key stages.

1. Acknowledging the hurt. (Calculating the debt)
2. Acknowledging how it made me feel.
3. Releasing the person from the perceived debt they owe me.
4. Accepting the person, just as they are, and relieving the person of the responsibility to make me feel loved and accepted.
5. Being willing to interact and thereby be heard again.

———————————————

List any forgiveness, rejection, or bitterness you still may have after reading this book:

_____

_____

_____

_____

_____

CREATING A THERAPEUTIC CULTURE OF MEN

Presenter Comments

I hope you were empowered after reading these two powerful stories. Were you able to figure out the strategies toward declaring your FREEDOM? The first step involved participating in the exercises and praying over what was revealed. It is time for society to remove the stigma it has on trauma or on seeking professionals equipped to bring clarity to life-experiences. Joe and Bruce overcame their circumstances, and you too can, because every story is different. This book was written to present men, especially African-Americans, in a positive light and encourage them to be free. Use your power and authority and take your voice back; it has long been silenced. This tool is the first installment into creating a therapeutic culture of men. Therapeutic simply means, "Relating to the healing of disease." And the disease men need to be healed from is SILENCE. No longer will trauma be the disease stealing the voice of men in any community. FREEDOM reigns!

-Linda D. Lee

To learn more, visit her website at
www.1lindadlee.com or linktr.ee/1lindadlee

ABOUT THE AUTHORS

Linda D. Lee

Linda D. Lee is the CEO and Founder of the LL Media Group, LLC, a Personal Development Consultancy company. She is a Professional Certified Life Coach, Certified Christian Mentor, International Speaker, Personal Development Consultant, Award-winning author, and a voice for the voiceless. She has amassed over 20 years combined experience in personal development, customer service, and emotion management strategies.

With her years of experience and wealth of revelatory knowledge, she touches lives through the creation of workshops and webinars to build healthy relationship competencies, virtually or physically, as a *Family Relationship Midwife.* ®

As a prolific writer she has been labeled a 'Powerhouse Phenomenon' by Huffington Post, and has been featured on the internationally syndicated platforms KHVN Heaven 97, The Cedric Bailey Show, Immerss TV, I Am Princess of Suburbia TV, *I Am A Storyteller Magazine*, *Queen "B" Magazine*, Access 34 TV, The Ricardo Miller Show, Stellar Award Candidate 'Big Mouth' Radio Show, *Modern Citizen Magazine*,

Today's Purpose Woman Magazine, YOU Magazine, Divine Inspiration Magazine, and others.

Linda garnered respect and admiration as she facilitated workshops and undertook speaking engagements in Cape Coast, Ghana, Africa, and London, UK, with a new collaboration in Mozambique, Africa.

To learn more, visit her website at
www.1lindadlee.com or linktr.ee/1lindadlee

FREEDOM

Joe J. Bridgewater

Joe J. Bridgewater is a retired Master Sergeant from the United States Air Force. He is also a retired mechanic, a former Sunday school teacher, and a church trustee. He is a loving husband, father, brother, uncle, grandfather, and great grandfather. He endured many struggles and obstacles to get to this 'overcomers book'. Although he learned to appreciate everything God allowed him to experience, he still had one question.

He has always been a soft-spoken person who loved to help others. Joe has spent countless hours volunteering servant leadership to the Boy Scouts of America, with faith-based organizations, and with many youth achievement events.

At one point in his life he wondered, 'Why am I still here?' Unbeknownst to him, a divine revelation was unfolding, even as he agreed to share his riveting story. He broke his SILENCE in order to free another man bound by his past. Joe is looking forward to many more people being freed from their shackles as a result of 'FREEDOM'. Now man will no longer suffer in silence. The stigma has been removed and counseling is no longer a myth for men. He is humbled to be a part of the creation of a therapeutic culture of men, for now, and for many generations to come.

CREATING A THERAPEUTIC CULTURE OF MEN

Bruce Lee

Bruce Lee is the CEO and founder of Young Soldiers for Christ, a child development ministry focused on enriching today's youth, academically and socially, providing them with competencies to ensure a successful future. He has been a motivational and inspirational speaker at several professional alliances, networks and conferences, including the Steve Harvey Mentoring Camp for Young Men, Regional and National Ministers Roundtable of Texas, Reaching Teens, and the My Brother's Keeper Initiative, created under a mandate issued by President Obama.

Bruce brings to the community over 30 years of first-hand experience and education in business management and child psychology. He works in collaboration with school administrators, teachers, and community activists in developing structured programs for educational growth. He also provides guidance to young men and young ladies through rehabilitative intervention programs that empower individual development. As such, he is a recipient of the Minority Leaders Citizen Council Award for his phenomenal work in the community.

He has a passion for teaching children and believes, "… speaking life into them," will change their lives.

www.ingramcontent.com/pod-product-compliance
Lightning Source LLC
LaVergne TN
LVHW051152080426
835508LV00021B/2593